GABRIEL, GOD, AND THE FUZZY BLANKET

For Mom and Dad, who lived their faith and passed it along to me. Thanks, with much love.
—A.G.

To Shelby and Marion, whose spacious house is almost as grand as their faith. Thank you, Marion.
—D.E.

Text Copyright © 2000 by Annette Griessman
Illustrations Copyright © 2000 by David L. Erickson

Morehouse Publishing
P.O. Box 1321
Harrisburg, PA 17105

Morehouse Publishing is a division of The Morehouse Group.

Printed in Malaysia

Cover design by Laurie Klein Westhafer

Library of Congress Cataloging-in-Publication Data

Griessman, Annette.
    Gabriel, God, and the fuzzy blanket / text by Annette Griessman; illustrations by David L. Erickson.
        p. cm.
    Summary: Jacob is afraid when he forgets to take his blanket on a visit to his great aunt and uncle, but his parents help him remember that God is always with him to keep him safe.
    ISBN 0-8192-1805-7 (alk. paper)
    [1. Blankets—Fiction. 2. Fear—Fiction. 3. Christian life—Fiction.]
I. Erickson, David L., 1964- ill. II Title.

PZ7.G881235 Gab 2000
[E]—dc21
                                                                        99-053212

GABRIEL, GOD, AND THE FUZZY BLANKET

Text by Annette Griessman

Illustrations by David L. Erickson

MOREHOUSE PUBLISHING

Jacob looked out of the car window and yawned. The trees outside were whipping by in a bright green blur. Jacob had hoped to see something more interesting than trees. They were going to Great Uncle Jack and Great Aunt Alice's house, and that was far away from home.

The trees just went on and on though, and he was tired. He reached out, feeling for the fuzzy softness that should be beside him… but felt only the cool slickness of the seat.

Jacob sat straight up, his eyes searching fearfully. He leaned out as far as he could and looked at the floor, hoping to see a familiar hint of blue. But there was none.

Then he remembered he had left it in the kitchen. He had put it down when his mom had given him the new truck to play with in the car. His breath seemed to catch in his throat as he cried, "Mom! I forgot my blanket. We have to go back!"

Jacob's mom peered back at him from the front seat. "Are you sure you don't have it, Hon?"

"No!" said Jacob. His eyes filled with tears. "I need my blanket. I need it!"

"We're two hours from home, Squirt," said Jacob's dad. "You have your truck. Play with that instead." Jacob could see his dad's eyes in the rearview mirror as he smiled at Jacob. But Jacob didn't smile back. He had to make them understand. He held his blanket close at night when the wind whistled through the trees. And when he was sad or lonely, he wrapped it tightly around his shoulders, like a warm, fuzzy hug. His blanket always made him feel better.

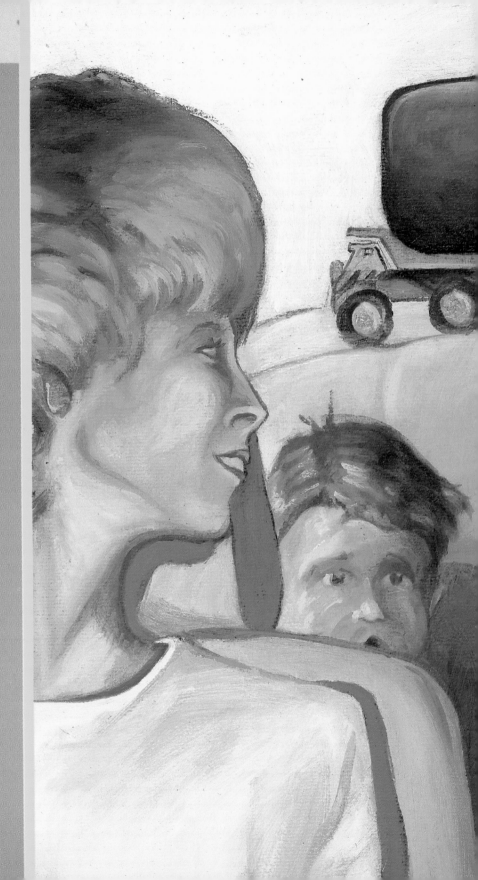

Jacob's mom held out her thick pink sweater. "Why don't you snuggle this, Hon? It's almost as fuzzy as your blanket." But his mother's sweater was not the same as Jacob's blanket—not at all. Jacob turned angrily toward the window, shoving his shiny, yellow truck and the sweater to the floor. He didn't want that stupid truck and he didn't want his mom's sweater. He wanted his blanket. The tears dripped slowly down his cheek as he stared at the blurry green trees.

Jacob was still angry when the car pulled into a long, gravel driveway. "We're here, Jacob," said his mom. Jacob's anger turned to fear as he stepped from the car. The house before him was big and white, with a high pointed roof. Knobby trees loomed nearby, their branches twisting out like long, thin fingers to touch the sides of the house. Jacob didn't want to go into this house—it was scary. He longed to clutch his blanket, to hold it close. Instead, he clung to his mom's skirt as they went up the steps and rang the bell.

Two of the oldest people Jacob had ever seen answered the door. Great Uncle Jack was very tall, with a long, gray beard and bushy eyebrows. Great Aunt Alice had wispy red hair and her hands shook. Jacob hid behind his mom.

"I am so glad you're here, Jacob!" said Great Aunt Alice, peering around at him. Her voice was loud and her eyes looked funny through her thick glasses. Jacob stayed behind his mom as the three of them went in the house.

A big, spotted dog bounded across the floor. It was as tall as Jacob, and had sharp, white teeth. Jacob screamed and pushed his way in between his mom and dad.

"Oh, that's just Gabriel, Jacob!" said Great Aunt Alice. "He won't hurt you. He's as gentle as a lamb."

Jacob didn't believe her. If he had his blanket, he would have shooed it at that dog and chased it away. But he didn't, so he stayed close to his mom—as far from the dog as he could get.

Jacob was still clinging to his mom at bedtime. "What's wrong, Hon?" she asked as she tucked him in. "You don't seem like you're having any fun here." Jacob shook his head. He wasn't having any fun here. Things here were scary and strange. He didn't like the bed—the mattress was lumpy—and the room smelled of dust. Cobwebs hung from the cracked ceiling.

Jacob pulled the covers up. "I need my blanket, Mom. I can't sleep without it!"

They both looked up as Jacob's dad stepped into the room. "Are you afraid without your blanket, Jacob? Is that it?" his dad asked gently. Jacob felt his chin tremble.

"Y–yes," he whispered.

His dad and mom sat on the edge of the bed. "You know, Jacob," said his dad, taking Jacob's hand. "There is someone who can help you with your fear better than your blanket."

Jacob frowned. "Who? You and Mom?"

"We're always here to help, Jacob," said his dad. "But actually I was thinking of God. God is always with you, you know. Remember the Bible verse you learned in Sunday school? 'Be not frightened... for the Lord your God is with you wherever you go.'"

Jacob bit his lip worriedly. He knew God was with him—but he wanted to feel cozy and comfortable, just like he felt when he held his blanket.

"Why don't we pray and tell God what's bothering you, okay? We'll ask for His help," said his mom.

Jacob wasn't sure this was going to work, but he leaned against his mother and closed his eyes in prayer.

His mom wrapped her arms around him and folded her hands. His dad folded his hands and leaned close. "Dear God," began his mother, "Jacob is awfully scared here in this new place. You said we shouldn't be afraid—that you are always with us. Please be with Jacob and help him sleep without his blanket tonight. Amen."

"Did that help, Squirt?" said his dad. Jacob could see in their eyes that he was supposed to say yes. His eyes darted around the room. Everything looked just the same—scary and strange. But he nodded anyway. His mom and dad both looked so certain that everything was fine.

After they left, Jacob lay in the darkness, his eyes wide. He was still very afraid. The floor in the hallway creaked and Jacob jumped. He ducked under the covers, wishing he had his blanket. When he poked his head out, the dog was standing in the doorway, staring at him. Trembling, Jacob stared back, trying to remember that God was with him and would help him be less afraid.

Jacob took a deep, shaky breath and looked at the dog more closely. He had to admit that Gabriel didn't really look mean. His teeth were big, but his eyes were a nice, warm, friendly brown. Jacob felt his fear fade a little. Slowly he sat up and whispered, "Hello, Gabriel." Gabriel whined softly and took a step closer. The dog was trying to tell him something, thought Jacob. "What do you want, Gabriel?" he said to the dog.

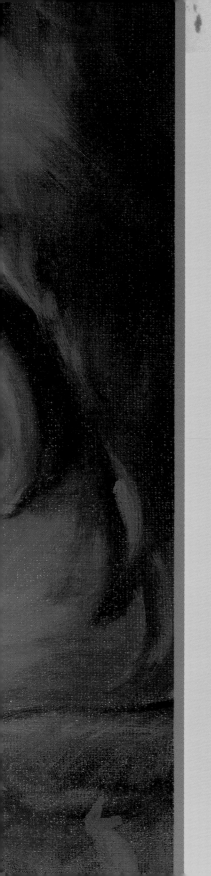

Gabriel stepped so close that Jacob could feel his warm breath on his arm. Then Gabriel laid his head on the bed. Jacob blinked, wondering what to do. Slowly he held out a hand.

Gabriel opened his mouth, and Jacob swallowed hard. The teeth were really long and sharp, but Jacob didn't pull back. Then the pink, wet tongue shot out... and licked Jacob's hand. That tongue tickled. Jacob smiled. He might not have his blanket, but he had a new friend. The last of Jacob's fear faded away. The next thing he knew, Gabriel was curled up beside him on the bed. Soon, the two of them fell contentedly to sleep.

Sunlight shone into Jacob's eyes and he blinked. Gabriel was still curled up beside him, and Jacob patted the dog's furry head. Jacob had been able to sleep in this strange room all night with Gabriel, who was not mean at all. Best of all, Jacob had been able to sleep without his blanket.

Later that morning, Jacob found out that Great Aunt Alice made the best pancakes he had ever eaten. And Great Uncle Jack could make kites that really flew. That afternoon, Jacob actually hated to leave. He was having a wonderful time.

"You come back soon, Jacob!" called Great Aunt Alice as their car pulled away. Jacob waved. He couldn't wait to come back.

That night, Jacob climbed into his own bed, in his own room. Clutched tightly to his side was his blue, fuzzy blanket. It felt good to have it close, and it still made him feel cozy and calm. But Jacob now knew that God could help him more than his blanket.

After all, you could forget to take a blanket with you, he thought, but you could never forget to take God.

Jacob smiled and went to sleep.